just

GARLIC.

just

A LITTLE BOOK OF AROMATIC ADVENTURES

GARLIC.

The Editors of Lyons Press

Lyons Press
Guilford, Connecticut

An imprint of Globe Pequot Press

Copyright © 2011 by Morris Book Publishing, LLC

Lyons Press is an imprint of Globe Pequot Press.

Library of Congress Cataloging-in-Publication Data is available on file.

ISBN 978-1-59921-938-7

The information in this book is true and complete to the best of our knowledge. All recommendations are made without guarantee on the part of Globe Pequot Press. Globe Pequot Press disclaims any liability in connection with the use of this information.

Printed in China

10 9 8 7 6 5 4 3 2 1

CONTENTS

Introduction vii

Garlic Basics 1

Appetizers 8

Poultry 32

Beef and Pork 52

Seafood 70

Side Dishes 89

Resources .108

Glossary 112

Metric Conversion Table 115

Index 116

Bad breath aside, garlic is one of the most versatile culinary ingredients available.

Originally discovered in central Asia thousands of years ago, garlic has played a prominent role in Mediterranean dishes for ages, but it is a relative newcomer to American cuisine, having just become popular in the States in the early twentieth century.

The love affair with garlic has since spread and it is now cultivated globally, with China producing nearly 23 billion pounds of garlic annually. Most of the garlic grown domestically is from Gilroy, California, dubbed the Garlic Capital of the World.

A close relative to the onion, garlic is a member of the Alliaceae family and serves as many culinary functions as it does medicinal. Garlic has been credited with being rich in antioxidants and preventing gangrene, heart disease, cancer, and staving off the common cold. In terms of culinary appeal, garlic blends well with almost anything. It is an excellent food that can be used to replace the salt flavor in many foods and once cooked, its mellow flavor is a perfect complement to seafood, pork, poultry, beef, vegetables, soups, stews, and sauces.

Many people shy away from the pungent food because of its reputation for leaving behind bad breath and smelly fingertips. While raw garlic has a strong taste, when cooked it is mild and leaves no trace on the breath. And removing the garlicky smell from hands is simple: rub them against a stainless steel surface, such as a sink or faucet, for 30 seconds and it will remove the unpleasant odor. Once you get over the inconvenience of its pungent smell, garlic is a wonderfully sweet addition to any dish.

So, whether you are looking to give your immune system a healthy boost, stimulate your taste buds, or ward off vampires, *Just Garlic* will have *just* the recipe for you ●

Inspect your garlic before purchasing, and be sure to buy hard cloves that are free of spots.

PEELING

The easiest way to peel garlic is to smash it. Put the clove on a cutting board; press the flat side of a chef's knife down on the garlic and apply pressure. The paper-like skin will break apart, allowing you to easily pull out the cloves. To prepare a lot of cloves at one time, spread them out on a piece of waxed paper. Add another layer of waxed paper on top of the garlic, then rock a heavy frying pan over the paper to smash. Once the garlic is smashed, it will peel easily and the split cloves will be ready to go into the cooking pan.

Other ways to loosen the skin include pouring hot water over the garlic cloves, soaking the cloves in cool water for 30 minutes, and zapping the cloves for five seconds in a microwave oven.

CHOPPING

Remove the skin by following the instructions for peeling above. Then cut the garlic into small pieces

using a chef's knife. For easier chopping of garlic, use a food processor. Just make sure you pulse to get an even chop. Note: A single clove of garlic is three times stronger in flavor if pressed through a garlic press than if chopped or diced.

MINCING

Smash each clove of garlic with the flat side of a chef's knife so that the paper skin can be removed easily. Use a garlic press, if available, to finely mince the garlic. If you do not have a garlic press, you can use a very sharp knife to slice each clove as thin as possible, and then finely chop until the garlic is minced. Adding a pinch of salt makes this process easier.

SAUTÉING

Garlic is sometimes referred to as an aromatic because of the sweet smell that emanates from it when put in contact with heat. To sauté garlic, use medium heat to cook in a sauté pan, and allow the garlic to soften and become golden. High heat can burn garlic. Remove from the pan before it gets brown.

ROASTING

Garlic becomes unbelievably sweet and mild when roasted. To roast a whole head of garlic, cut it in half and place in a 350°F oven for one hour, until soft. Remove from oven and let cool, then squeeze the garlic from the peel. Or you can serve the roasted garlic head all by itself, as a side dish to meat or as an appetizer. Let your guests remove the cloves from the heads and spread them directly on toasted bread or grilled steak.

It's easy to roast 6–7 heads of garlic at once, then remove the sweet meat from the skins and freeze. When you need to use it just remove the amount you need and defrost in the microwave. You can also roast

garlic in oil on the stovetop for 7–9 minutes until brown, then discard the oil and let the cloves cool.

STORING

Garlic keeps best when stored in a cool, dry place away from direct sunlight (not in the refrigerator!). Sometimes a garlic clove will sprout; this is normal. Use immediately and discard sprouted areas ●

Three-Onion Soup with Garlic

INGREDIENTS

3 tablespoons extra-virgin olive oil
4 large yellow onions, diced
4 leeks, carefully rinsed and diced
3 ounces pancetta, finely diced
5 garlic cloves
6 cups low-salt chicken stock
1¼ cups fruity red wine, such as Chianti or
  Zinfandel

2 tablespoons balsamic vinegar
1 tablespoon red wine vinegar
Salt and ground pepper
1 cup freshly grated Parmesan cheese

YIELD: 6 SERVINGS

1. In a soup pot over medium heat, warm the oil. Add the onions, leeks, and pancetta. Sauté, stirring occasionally, until the onions and leeks are soft, about 10 minutes.

2. Add the garlic and sauté, stirring, for 1 minute. Add the stock and wine; simmer, uncovered, over medium-low heat until the vegetables are very soft, about 30 minutes.

3. Just before serving, stir in the balsamic and red wine vinegars; season with salt and pepper.

4. Ladle the soup into bowls. Sprinkle with Parmesan cheese.

Roasted Garlic Tortilla Soup

INGREDIENTS

2 cups chicken stock
2 cloves garlic
$1/2$ cup chopped canned tomatoes with juice
$1/2$ cup canned black beans, drained and rinsed
$1/2$ cup canned corn kernels, drained and rinsed
1 teaspoon cumin
$1/2$ cup finely chopped fresh cilantro
Juice of $1/2$ lime
1 cup cubed cooked chicken
$1/2$ cup slightly crushed baked tortilla chips
1 dollop low-fat sour cream

YIELD: 2 SERVINGS

1. Pour the chicken stock into a large pot.

2. Over medium-high heat, bring the chicken stock to a boil. Reduce the heat, and let the stock simmer. Roast garlic on the stovetop (see pages 5–6), then mince.

3. Add the garlic, tomatoes, beans, corn, and cumin to the pot. Simmer 10–15 minutes, then add cilantro, lime juice, and chicken.

4. Simmer another 5–10 minutes, then remove from heat.

5. Prepare a bowl with chips by dumping crushed tortilla chips into a soup bowl. Pour a cup of the soup over the chips and finish with a dollop of sour cream.

Roasted Garlic Herb Spread

INGREDIENTS

2 tablespoons olive oil
8 cloves garlic
2 teaspoons lemon juice
$1/2$ teaspoon salt
$1/8$ teaspoon pepper
1 cup cubed Brie cheese
$1/2$ cup low-fat sour cream
2 tablespoons butter

YIELD: 8 SERVINGS

1. Place oil in small pan over medium heat. Add garlic cloves; cook, watching carefully, until cloves turn brown.

2. You can also roast the whole head, cut in half, in a 350°F oven for 1 hour until soft.

3. Remove garlic from oil and let cool, then squeeze garlic from peel. Combine garlic with lemon juice, salt, and pepper.

4. In food processor, combine garlic mixture with remaining ingredients; process until smooth. Cover and chill for 2–3 hours before serving.

Rich Artichoke Garlic Dip

INGREDIENTS

2 tablespoons butter
1 leek, chopped
4 cloves garlic, minced
16-ounce package frozen cut leaf spinach,
  thawed and drained
2 (14-ounce) cans artichoke hearts, drained and
  chopped
1 cup mayonnaise
16-ounce jar Alfredo sauce or 2 cups white sauce
1$1/2$ cups shredded Havarti cheese
$3/4$ cup grated Parmesan cheese, divided

YIELD: 8 SERVINGS

1. Melt butter in medium skillet or stovetop-
   proof 3$1/2$-quart slow cooker. Cook leek and
   garlic until tender.

2. In slow cooker, combine leek mixture
   with remaining ingredients except $1/2$ cup
   Parmesan cheese; mix well.

3. Cover and cook on low for 6–7 hours, or
   on high for 3–4 hours, stirring once during
   cooking time, until mixture bubbles.

4. Sprinkle with remaining $1/2$ cup Parmesan
   cheese and serve with crudités and crackers.

Roasted Garlic Dip

INGREDIENTS

2 large heads garlic
2 tablespoons olive oil
1 onion, chopped
1 tablespoon unsalted butter
3 tablespoons lemon juice
1 cup canned cannellini beans
$1/2$ cup sour cream
1 tablespoon minced fresh rosemary leaves
$1/8$ teaspoon pepper

YIELD: 8 SERVINGS

1. Cut garlic heads in half crosswise, through the equator. Place, cut side up, on baking sheet; drizzle with olive oil.

2. Roast garlic at 375°F for 50–60 minutes, until browned. Remove cloves from skin.

3. Cook onion in butter until very tender, about 6–7 minutes.

4. In food processor place garlic cloves, onion, lemon juice, beans, and remaining ingredients; process until smooth. Chill.

Be sure that all the papery skin is removed from the garlic flesh, or it will create an unpleasant texture.

You can process this dip until smooth or leave some small pieces of garlic and beans for some texture.

Add herbs to this dip for more flavor. Thyme, marjoram, basil, and oregano are all good choices.

Roasted Chile Salsa
with Garlic

INGREDIENTS

1 pound large, fresh red chiles such as Anaheim
1 red bell pepper
1 onion, cut into quarters
6 garlic cloves, peeled
1 pound ripe tomatoes
1 cup cilantro leaves
3 tablespoons vinegar
1 teaspoon salt

YIELD: 4–6 SERVINGS

1. Roast the chiles and bell pepper until the skins are blackened. Peel the skins off and remove the stems and seeds.

2. Place the onion quarters, garlic, and tomatoes onto a baking sheet and brown them under a broiler.

3. Let the tomatoes cool, cut the stem area out, and use a spoon to scoop out the majority of the seeds and liquid.

4. Place all the ingredients into a food processor and process until combined. The salsa should have some texture, it should not be completely smooth. You can enjoy the salsa immediately or let rest in the refrigerator overnight, allowing the flavors to blend. Serve with tortilla chips or use as a topping for tacos or a sauce for burritos.

If fresh red chiles are not available, substitute fresh green chiles such as New Mexico or poblano chiles. The green chiles will give the salsa a more muted neutral color rather than a bright red tone, but it will still have excellent flavor.

APPETIZERS

Pico de Gallo

INGREDIENTS

6 Roma or plum tomatoes
½ medium white onion
1 jalapeño
5 cloves garlic
1 handful cilantro leaves
2 tablespoons fresh lime juice
½ teaspoon salt

YIELD: 8 SERVINGS

1. Dice the tomatoes, discarding the majority of the seeds and juice. Add them to a large bowl.

2. Chop the onion and add it to the tomatoes. Seed and dice the jalapeño and add it to the bowl.

3. After removing the garlic skins, chop the garlic and cilantro, and add them to the bowl.

4. Sprinkle with lime juice and salt, toss ingredients to combine. Serve with tortilla chips.

Fresh and flavorful ingredients are the keys to delicious pico de gallo. If you use bland or old produce, your finished product will lack flavor and color. Purchase your ingredients no more than two to three days before you make the recipe so that they are as fresh as possible. To bring out even more flavor, let pico de gallo rest in the refrigerator for about an hour.

Bruschetta

INGREDIENTS

6 slices crusty Italian bread, about 1 inch thick
2–3 garlic cloves, peeled
Extra-virgin olive oil
Freshly ground black pepper

YIELD: 6 SERVINGS

1. Grill the bread slices on an outdoor grill, or toast in an oven on a baking sheet, until nicely browned on both sides, about 5 minutes.

2. Rub each slice, on one side only, with a whole clove of garlic.

3. Place each bread slice on an individual serving plate, and drizzle with extra-virgin olive oil.

4. Sprinkle freshly ground black pepper over the bread slices. Serve by itself or as an accompaniment to soup.

> The perfect bread for bruschetta is a crusty rustic type that can hold the fruity oil and the variety of toppings.

Pickled Carrots with Garlic

INGREDIENTS

5 cloves garlic
1 pound peeled carrots
2 tablespoons cooking oil
3/4 cup vinegar
5 bay leaves
5 peppercorns
1/2 teaspoon salt
3/4 cup water
1/4 cup pickled jalapeños with the canning juice

YIELD: 6 CUPS

1. Peel and chop the garlic cloves. Peel and cut the carrots on the diagonal about 1/4-inch thick.

2. Heat the oil in a large pan and sauté the garlic and carrots 2–3 minutes.

3. Slowly add the vinegar, bay leaves, peppercorns, and salt and bring to a simmer 5 minutes.

4. Add the water and jalapeños and simmer an additional 10 minutes. Remove bay leaves, cool the mixture and store in the refrigerator in an airtight container overnight for maximum flavor. Serve using a slotted spoon, leaving liquid behind.

Before beginning this recipe, assemble all of your supplies and prepare the garlic and carrots. Measure out all the liquids and have them ready to add. If you measure as you go, there is more room for error. Getting everything ready first cuts down on the overall time it takes to prepare a recipe.

Garlic Curried Wings

INGREDIENTS

2 tablespoons olive oil
2 cloves garlic, minced
2 shallots, minced
1 tablespoon curry powder
$1/4$ cup lemon juice
$1/2$ teaspoon salt
$1/8$ teaspoon pepper
$1/3$ cup honey
$1^1/2$ pounds chicken wings, prepared

YIELD: 6–8 SERVINGS

1. In small saucepan, heat olive oil. Add garlic, shallots, and curry powder; cook 4 minutes; remove from heat.

2. Add lemon juice, salt, pepper, and honey. Place wings in baking dish; pour sauce over. Refrigerate 6–24 hours.

3. Reserve marinade; place wings on broiler pan; broil 6 inches from heat source 15 minutes, turning frequently.

4. Brush wings with reserved marinate; continue broiling, turning, and basting, 10–15 minutes longer until done. These wings can be served hot or cold. The glaze will form a slightly chewy, sweet, and tart crust on the wings. To serve cold, cover and chill them for 4–5 hours before serving.

Broiling wings is a delicious way to get crisp skin and tender meat with little fuss or mess. You need to be careful when broiling wings because they will pop and spatter under the intense heat. Always use potholders to protect your hands and arms when turning wings under the broiler.

Garlic Wings Casino

INGREDIENTS

4 slices bacon
1 tablespoon butter
2 pounds chicken wings, each cut into 3 pieces,
  tips discarded
¼ cup dry white wine
1 onion, finely chopped
4 cloves garlic, minced
1 green bell pepper, chopped
¼ cup chicken broth
1 tablespoon lemon juice
⅓ cup grated Parmesan cheese

YIELD: 6 SERVINGS

1. Cook bacon until crisp in large skillet; drain,
   crumble, and set aside. Remove all but 2
   tablespoons drippings.

2. Add butter; brown wings on both sides;
   remove wings to baking dish; drizzle with
   wine.

3. Bake wings at 375°F 30–40 minutes.
   Meanwhile, add onion, garlic, and bell pepper
   to skillet; cook 5 minutes.

4. Add broth and lemon juice; simmer 5
   minutes. When wings are done, top each

with a spoonful of vegetables, bacon, and cheese. Bake 10 minutes longer.

These wings are delicious served with a glass of dry white wine before a meal of grilled steak or salmon, along with a spinach salad. For dessert, a lemon meringue pie would be perfect.

Chicken with 40 Cloves of Garlic

INGREDIENTS

1 (4-pound) roasting chicken
2 tablespoons butter
$\frac{1}{2}$ teaspoon salt
$\frac{1}{8}$ teaspoon white pepper
$\frac{1}{2}$ teaspoon paprika
$\frac{1}{2}$ lemon
1 fresh sprig of thyme
1 fresh sprig of oregano
3 stems fresh flat-leaf parsley
$\frac{1}{4}$ cup chopped celery leaves
$\frac{1}{4}$ cup olive oil
$\frac{1}{2}$ cup chicken broth

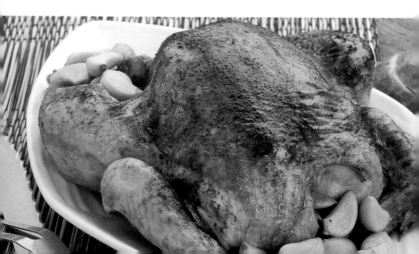

¼ cup dry white wine
40 cloves garlic, unpeeled

YIELD: 4 SERVINGS

1. Pat chicken dry and rub outside with butter. Sprinkle with salt, pepper, and paprika.

2. Stuff chicken with a lemon half, thyme, oregano, parsley, and celery leaves, then place in large roasting pan.

3. Add olive oil, broth, and wine to pan and add garlic. Cover with foil and place in 375°F. oven.

4. Roast for 90 minutes, then uncover and roast 15-20 minutes longer until chicken registers 180°F. Remove chicken and garlic from pan and serve.

To get 40 cloves of garlic, you'll need about 3 whole heads. Separate the cloves from the head with your fingers. Discard excess papery covering by making a small cut with a knife, then pulling off the skin. You can peel the garlic or leave it unpeeled. If it's peeled it will become softer than unpeeled garlic.

The garlic can be served with the chicken, stirred into mashed potatoes or rice pilaf, or just piled on a plate. In that case, offer some warm French bread and tell your guests to smash the soft garlic onto the bread.

Roast Lemon-Garlic Chicken

INGREDIENTS

1 (3-pound) roasting chicken
2 lemons, sliced
4 cloves garlic, crushed
3 tablespoons unsalted butter
1 teaspoon paprika
$\frac{1}{2}$ teaspoon dry mustard
$\frac{1}{4}$ teaspoon garlic powder
$\frac{1}{4}$ teaspoon white pepper
3 tablespoons lemon juice

YIELD: 4 SERVINGS

1. Rinse chicken and pat dry. Preheat oven to 350°F.

2. Place half of the sliced lemons in roasting pan. Top with chicken. Place remaining lemon slices in cavity of chicken along with garlic.

3. In saucepan, melt butter; add paprika, mustard, garlic powder, pepper, and lemon juice. Pour half over chicken.

4. Roast chicken 30 minutes, then baste with remaining butter mixture. Roast 40–45 minutes longer, until chicken registers 180°F. Cover and let stand 15 minutes; slice to serve.

For even more flavor and to release more juice, roll the lemons on the countertop before you slice them. The garlic should be crushed with the side of a chef's knife. You can leave the peel on.

The lemons and garlic in the cavity of the chicken are just for flavor. They won't look pretty when the chicken is done, so don't remove them. Just carve the chicken at the table and leave these ingredients in the cavity.

Spatchcocked Grilled Chicken with Garlic Marinade

INGREDIENTS

6 cloves garlic, minced
2 teaspoons salt
$1/2$ teaspoon pepper
$1/2$ teaspoon garlic powder
2 teaspoons paprika
$1/4$ cup olive oil
2 tablespoons butter
1 (3–4-pound) whole chicken

YIELD: 4–6 SERVINGS

1. Mix garlic with salt, pepper, garlic powder, paprika, oil, and butter.

2. With kitchen shears or sharp knife, cut the backbone out of the chicken. Place chicken, bone side down, on work surface. Press down on the chicken breast to flatten chicken.

3. Loosen skin and rub on half of the garlic mixture under skin. Smooth skin over flesh and rub in remaining mixture.

4. Refrigerate for 8–12 hours. Grill chicken, skin side down, on direct medium heat for 15 minutes. Turn; grill for 20–25 minutes longer until 170°F.

Spatchcock sounds like such a fancy English term. It actually originated in Ireland. All it means is a chicken with its backbone removed so it will lay flat on the grill; it's a butterflied chicken.

Garlic Chicken Paprikash

INGREDIENTS

1 (4-pound) whole chicken, cut into serving
   pieces
1/3 cup flour
1 teaspoon salt
1/4 teaspoon cayenne pepper
2 tablespoons paprika, divided
1 tablespoon butter
2 tablespoons olive oil

1 onion, chopped
4 cloves garlic, minced
1½ cups chicken broth
3 tomatoes, peeled, seeded, and diced
1 cup sour cream

YIELD: 6 SERVINGS

1. Pat chicken dry. Combine flour, salt, pepper, and 2 teaspoons paprika; dredge chicken.

2. Melt butter and olive oil in large pan. Brown chicken, skin side down, removing from pan as it cooks.

3. Add onion and garlic; cook 4 minutes. Add chicken with remaining paprika, broth, and tomatoes.

4. Cover and simmer for 60–70 minutes until chicken registers 170°F; remove chicken. Add spoonful of juices to sour cream; return to sauce; cook until thickened. Serve with medium or wide egg noodles to soak up the delicious sauce.

Garlic Chicken Casserole

INGREDIENTS

8 boneless, skinless chicken thighs, cut into
  strips
3 tablespoons flour
1 teaspoon paprika
Salt and pepper to taste
2 tablespoons butter
1 onion, chopped
5 cloves garlic, minced
1 cup uncooked long-grain rice
2 red bell peppers, chopped
1 (4-ounce) jar pimentos, drained
1 teaspoon dried thyme leaves
$1/8$ teaspoon cinnamon
3 cups chicken stock
2 tomatoes, peeled, seeded, and chopped
$1/3$ cup ground almonds
1 cup shredded Manchego cheese, divided
$1/3$ cup sliced black olives

YIELD: 6 SERVINGS

1. Dredge chicken in flour, paprika, salt, and
   pepper. Melt butter in saucepan. Add
   chicken; brown on all sides; remove.

2. Add onion and garlic to pan; stir to remove
   drippings. Add rice; cook 3–4 minutes. Add
   bell peppers and pimentos; cook 3–4 minutes.

3. Add thyme, cinnamon, and stock; simmer, covered, for 15 minutes. Add chicken, tomatoes, almonds, and ½ cup cheese.

4. Pour into 2½-quart casserole. Top with remaining cheese and olives. Bake, covered, at 375°F 35–40 minutes.

You can make this recipe with boneless, skinless chicken breasts as well. Bake the casserole for 25–30 minutes until bubbly and hot.

Chicken Adobo with Garlic

INGREDIENTS

1 (3-pound) frying chicken, cut into serving
  pieces
¼ cup soy sauce
¼ cup white vinegar
¼ cup red wine vinegar
2 tablespoons brown sugar
⅓ cup coconut milk
2 cups chicken broth
10 cloves garlic, minced

2 onions, chopped
2 bay leaves
1/8 teaspoon cayenne pepper
1/8 teaspoon pepper
1 1/2 cups long-grain white rice

YIELD: 4 SERVINGS

1. Place chicken in 4- or 5-quart slow cooker. In bowl, mix soy sauce, white vinegar, red wine vinegar, and brown sugar.

2. Add remaining ingredients except rice and mix well. Pour vinegar mixture over the chicken.

3. Cover and cook on low for 7–9 hours until chicken is very tender. Remove chicken and place in a 375°F oven; bake to crisp skin while preparing rice.

4. Pour 3 cups liquid into pan; add rice. Simmer 15–20 minutes until rice is tender; serve with chicken.

Adobo is the Spanish word for "marinade" or "sauce." There are many varieties of this recipe in the Spanish cultures.

Lemon-Garlic Grilled Hens

INGREDIENTS

1 onion, chopped
3 cloves garlic, minced
$\frac{1}{4}$ cup olive oil
$\frac{1}{3}$ cup lemon juice
2 teaspoons grated lemon zest
2 tablespoons honey
1 teaspoon salt
$\frac{1}{4}$ teaspoon pepper
1 teaspoon dried basil
1 teaspoon dried oregano
4 Cornish game hens

YIELD: 4 SERVINGS

1. In saucepan, cook onion and garlic in olive oil until tender. Let cool 15 minutes, then place in food processor.

2. Add lemon juice, zest, honey, salt, pepper, basil, and oregano and process until smooth; pour into large pan or bowl.

3. Add hens; turn to coat. Cover and marinate in fridge 8–24 hours.

4. Drain hens; reserve marinade. Grill over medium heat 55–65 minutes, brushing with remaining marinade, until 170°F. Let stand 10 minutes; discard remaining marinade.

When you're preparing the grill to cook whole Cornish hens, make sure to build a graduated fire, or prepare an indirect fire with a drip pan in place of some of the coals. The hens will probably need to be moved around on the grill so they don't overcook or burn.

Roasted Garlic Cornish Hens

INGREDIENTS

3 tablespoons butter
6 cloves garlic, minced
1½ teaspoons salt, divided
6 Cornish game hens
2 tablespoons olive oil
¼ teaspoon pepper
1 teaspoon paprika
1 teaspoon dried thyme leaves
2 lemons, sliced, divided

12 cloves garlic, whole
6 sprigs thyme
1 cup dry white wine

YIELD: 6 SERVINGS

1. Melt butter in pan; add minced garlic; cook 3 minutes.

2. Remove from heat and add $^3/_4$ teaspoon salt. Loosen skin from hens; rub mixture under skin; smooth skin back over flesh.

3. Drizzle hens with olive oil; sprinkle with remaining salt, pepper, paprika, and dried thyme.

4. Place half of lemon slices, whole garlic, and thyme in cavity. Place remaining lemons on hens; pour wine over. Roast at 350°F 55–65 minutes. Baste the hens at least once during cooking time. When the hens come out of the oven, cover to keep warm and let stand for 10–15 minutes to let the juices redistribute.

Most Cornish hens are sold frozen. Defrost according to the package directions, or thaw in the refrigerator for 24 hours.

If you find fresh hens, use or freeze them within 1 day, as they are very perishable.

Lemon-Garlic Roasted Turkey

INGREDIENTS

1 (11–12-pound) whole turkey
3 tablespoons lemon juice
1 tablespoon lemon zest
⅓ cup butter, softened
2 teaspoons dried thyme leaves
2 teaspoons salt
½ teaspoon pepper
4 cloves garlic, minced
2 lemons, cut in half
3 sprigs thyme
3 onions, sliced
3 carrots, sliced lengthwise
3 cups chicken stock

YIELD: 8-10 SERVINGS

1. Remove giblets, neck from turkey; cover parts with water and simmer for gravy.

2. Mix lemon juice, zest, butter, thyme, salt, pepper, and garlic. Rub the cavity under the skin, and on skin. Place lemon halves and thyme sprigs in cavity.

3. Using a grill, sear turkey on each side over direct medium heat for 10 minutes. Place onions and carrots in heavy duty roasting

pan; place on indirect medium heat. Add turkey and chicken stock.

4. Cover; grill for 2½–3 hours, or until meat thermometer in thigh registers 180°F. Let the turkey stand, covered, for 15 minutes to let the juices redistribute. Place the turkey on a large platter decorated with lemon slices and sprigs of thyme.

For a charcoal grill, you'll have to add 10–15 briquettes per hour to keep the heat consistent. Start the coals in your chimney starter for best results.

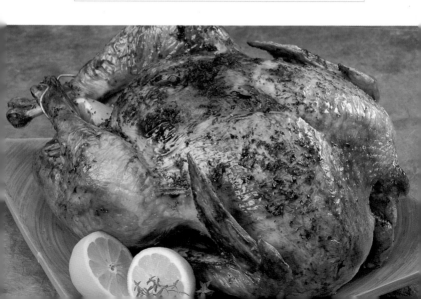

Rib Eye with Roasted Garlic Butter

INGREDIENTS

6 cloves garlic
2 tablespoons olive oil
$1/2$ teaspoon salt
$1/8$ teaspoon pepper
$1/3$ cup butter, softened
$1/4$ cup crumbled blue cheese
1 teaspoon chopped fresh oregano
4 boneless rib eye steaks

1 teaspoon grill seasoning

¼ teaspoon pepper

YIELD: 4 SERVINGS

1. Place unpeeled garlic cloves and oil in a small saucepan. Heat over medium heat until cloves turn golden brown.

2. Remove cloves from oil and let cool. Squeeze flesh from cloves. Combine with salt, pepper, butter, blue cheese, and oregano in small bowl; refrigerate.

3. Preheat grill to medium. Brush steaks with the oil from the garlic and sprinkle with grill seasoning and pepper.

4. Grill steaks over medium direct heat, turning at least twice, about 12–14 minutes for medium rare. Top with compound butter; serve immediately.

> You can form the compound butter into a log and chill, then cut rounds to top the steaks.
>
> Or just place the butter in a dish and spoon a dollop onto each steak for a more casual presentation.

Grilled Steak with Garlic-Lemon Paste

INGREDIENTS

4 (6- to 8-ounce) rib eye steaks
4 cloves garlic, minced
1 teaspoon paprika
1/4 teaspoon pepper
1 tablespoon lemon juice
1 teaspoon dried marjoram
2 tablespoons unsalted butter

YIELD: 4 SERVINGS

1. Let steaks stand at room temperature 15 minutes. Meanwhile, combine garlic, paprika, and pepper; mash into a paste.

2. Stir lemon juice and marjoram into garlic paste. Rub on steaks, both sides; let stand 15 minutes.

3. Prepare and preheat grill. Place steaks on rack 6 inches from medium coals; cover grill.

4. Grill without moving 5 minutes, then turn. Grill, covered, 6–10 minutes, until desired doneness. Remove; top with butter and cover. Let stand 5 minutes, then serve.

Sliced Beef with Garlic and Leeks

INGREDIENTS

1 pound sirloin or flank steak
2 tablespoons soy sauce, divided
2 tablespoons rice wine, divided
1 teaspoon Szechwan peppercorns, lightly
  toasted in dry wok and ground
1 tablespoon cornstarch
2–3 tablespoons vegetable oil
3 large leeks, julienned
6 cloves garlic, minced
1/2 teaspoon sugar
2 tablespoons fermented black beans
2 teaspoons sesame oil
1 teaspoon chile paste
Salt, to taste

YIELD: 4-6 SERVINGS

1. Thinly slice beef across the grain. Marinate
   30 minutes with 1 tablespoon soy sauce,
   1 tablespoon wine, toasted ground
   peppercorns, and cornstarch.

2. Stir-fry beef over high heat in vegetable oil;
   remove when cooked through.

3. Add julienned leeks and garlic to wok; stir-fry 1 minute. Remove a few leeks for garnish. Return beef to wok.

4. Combine remaining ingredients. Pour over beef and leeks. Stir-fry 1 minute. Add salt and garnish with reserved leeks.

Hot and Spicy Short Ribs

INGREDIENTS

4 cloves garlic, minced
1 teaspoon salt
¼ teaspoon pepper
½ cup low-sodium soy sauce
½ cup barbecue sauce
2 tablespoons olive oil
¼ cup apple cider vinegar
3 tablespoons adobo sauce
1 tablespoon chili powder
3 pounds individual short ribs; membrane removed
2 cups hickory wood chips

YIELD: 6 SERVINGS

1. Mash together garlic and salt until paste forms; place in large bowl. Add remaining ingredients except ribs and chips.

2. Add the ribs and turn to coat with the sauce. Cover and chill for 4–5 hours.

3. Prepare grill for indirect medium heat. Remove ribs from marinade. Place ribs on direct heat; brown for 6–7 minutes, turning once.

4. Place wood chips in drip pan. Grill ribs, covered, over indirect heat for 90–130 minutes, brushing occasionally with sauce, until very tender.

Shredded Pork in Garlic Sauce

INGREDIENTS

4 dried wood ear mushrooms
1 pound boneless pork butt or loin
3 tablespoons soy sauce, divided
1 teaspoon sesame oil
1 egg white
4 teaspoons cornstarch
2 tablespoons rice wine vinegar
2 tablespoons sugar
1 tablespoon rice wine
2 teaspoons chile paste
6 tablespoons vegetable oil
4 cloves garlic, minced
1 cup matchstick-cut bamboo shoots
$^2/_3$ cup slivered water chestnuts
2 green onions, cut into shreds
Salt to taste

YIELD: 4–6 SERVINGS

1. Soak wood ears in hot water 30 minutes. Drain and cut into matchsticks. Prepare pork.

2. Start with well-chilled or partially frozen pork. Place pork on a work surface and cut across the grain into $1/4$-inch-thick slices.

3. Lay slices flat and cut into long $1/4$-inch-thick matchstick-style strips; place in a bowl.

4. Whisk together 1 teaspoon soy sauce, sesame oil, and egg white. Pour over pork and stir to blend completely.

5. Sprinkle 1 teaspoon cornstarch over pork and toss to coat. Cover and refrigerate 30 minutes.

6. Combine soy sauce not used for pork with vinegar, sugar, wine, and chile paste. Fry the pork in hot oil; remove along with all but 2 tablespoons oil.

7. Stir-fry garlic, wood ears, bamboo shoots, water chestnuts, and green onions 1 minute. Add sauce and cook until bubbly. Return pork; stir-fry 1 minute. Dissolve remaining cornstarch in 2 tablespoons cold water. Add to wok and stir-fry until mixture thickens. Add salt. Serve with fluffy white rice to cool the palate.

Stir-Fried Garlic Pork Tenderloin

INGREDIENTS

1 pound pork tenderloin, thinly sliced
3 tablespoons soy sauce, divided
1 tablespoon rice wine
1 teaspoon sugar
2 teaspoons cornstarch
2 tablespoons vegetable oil, divided
1 tablespoon water
½ pound shiitake mushrooms
2 cups baby bok choy

1 cup baby corn
1 red bell pepper
$^2/_3$ cup water chestnuts
4 garlic cloves, minced
Salt and pepper, to taste

YIELD: 4 SERVINGS

1. Place pork in a large bowl. In another bowl, whisk together 1 tablespoon soy sauce, wine, and sugar. Add to pork. Sprinkle with cornstarch; toss to coat. Refrigerate 30 minutes.

2. Place wok over high heat; add 1 tablespoon oil and 1 tablespoon water.

3. Add cut vegetables to wok; cover and steam 1 minute.

4. Remove cover from wok, allowing water to completely evaporate. Stir-fry vegetables 2 minutes. Remove to a platter.

5. Add 1 tablespoon oil to the wok. Add garlic cloves and pork slices; stir-fry just until pork is no longer pink.

6. Stir in remaining soy sauce. Return vegetables to wok; stir-fry until heated through. Add salt and pepper; serve immediately.

Garlic-Lemon Marinated Grilled Chops

INGREDIENTS

2 tablespoons Dijon mustard
3 tablespoons lemon juice
1 teaspoon grated lemon zest
1 tablespoon olive oil
3 cloves garlic, minced
¼ teaspoon pepper
1 teaspoon dried oregano
6 (6-ounce) 1-inch thick pork chops

YIELD: 6 SERVINGS

1. In a large heavy-duty plastic bag, combine mustard, lemon juice, zest, olive oil, garlic, pepper, and oregano.

2. Add pork chops; seal and massage to coat. Place in dish in refrigerator. Marinate 8–24 hours, turning twice.

3. Prepare and preheat grill. Remove chops from marinade; reserve marinade.

4. Grill chops 6 inches from medium coals 11–14 minutes, brushing once with reserved marinade and turning once, until temperature registers 150°F. Cover; let stand 5 minutes and serve.

Not all pork chops are created equal. Different cuts have more flavor and are more tender than others. The loin chops, because they are cut from a muscle that isn't frequently used, is more tender than rib or blade chops. Look for center-cut boneless pork chops for ease in preparation.

Herbed Pork Roast with Garlic

INGREDIENTS

1 stalk fresh rosemary
3 sprigs fresh thyme
1 (4-pound) boneless pork loin roast
6 cloves garlic, slivered
1 teaspoon paprika
¼ teaspoon pepper
¼ teaspoon dry mustard
2 tablespoons olive oil
2 onions, chopped
½ cup water

18 baby new red potatoes
1 (16-ounce) package baby carrots

YIELD: 8–10 SERVINGS

1. Break rosemary stalk into 1-inch pieces.
   Break thyme sprigs into 1-inch pieces.

2. Using a sharp knife, make holes in the pork
   roast; insert rosemary, thyme, and garlic
   slivers in a regular pattern.

3. Mix paprika, pepper, mustard, and oil; brush
   on roast. Place on onions in roasting pan; add
   water.

4. Roast at 350°F 50 minutes. Add potatoes
   and carrots; roast another 45–55 minutes,
   until 150°F. Cover roast; let stand 10 minutes,
   then slice.

> The secret to the best pork roast is to make
> sure it's not overcooked. Use a meat thermom-
> eter that is then set to the proper temperature,
> 150°F. Take the roast out of the oven and let
> stand 10 minutes, then carve and dig in.

BEEF AND PORK

Pork Roast with Garlic and Rosemary

INGREDIENTS

2 cups wood chips (for grilling)
1 cup water
3-pound boneless pork loin roast
5 cloves garlic, slivered
3 sprigs fresh rosemary, cut into 1-inch pieces
$1/3$ cup Dijon mustard
$1/3$ cup honey
$1/4$ cup apple cider vinegar
2 tablespoons olive oil
1 teaspoon salt
$1/8$ teaspoon pepper

YIELD: 8 SERVINGS

1. Soak wood chips in water. Meanwhile, make $1/2$-inch-deep holes about $1 1/2$ inches apart over top of roast.

2. Insert garlic slivers and rosemary sprigs into the holes in the meat.

3. Combine remaining ingredients. Rub over roast. Cover meat and leftover marinade and refrigerate for 12–18 hours.

4. Using a grill, brown roast over direct heat, about 5 minutes; place over drip pan filled with drained wood chips and cover. Roast

for 25–30 minutes per pound, brushing with leftover marinade. Let the roast stand for 10 minutes, covered, after it comes off the grill, then slice and serve.

When preparing this recipe, be sure that you cut the garlic into very thin slivers so it melts into the meat as it grills.

Easy Chili-Garlic Shrimp

INGREDIENTS

2 tablespoons fish sauce

2 tablespoons vegetable oil

2 tablespoons coconut milk

$1/2$–$1$$1/2$ teaspoons cayenne pepper

$1$$1/2$ heaping tablespoons brown sugar

$1/2$ teaspoon shrimp paste

3 cloves garlic, minced

Optional: 2 kaffir lime leaves, torn (stem and central vein removed)

Optional: 1 red chile, minced, OR $1/2$ teaspoon dried chile flakes (for extra-hot shrimp)

18–20 medium to large raw shrimp (thawed if frozen)

To serve: Lemon or lime wedges and fresh coriander

1. Place the fish sauce, oil, coconut milk, cayenne pepper, brown sugar, shrimp paste, garlic, and lime leaves (if using) in a mini chopper or food processor. Process well to create a fragrant marinade.

2. Remove shells from shrimp except for the tails. Butterfly the shrimp by making a cut down the length of the back. Avoid cutting too deeply: $1/4$–$1/3$ inch is deep enough. Remove any veins and rinse under cold water.

3. Place prepared shrimp in a bowl and pour the marinade over, tossing to coat. Marinate 5 minutes (avoid over-marinating shellfish: 10 minutes maximum).

4. Turn oven to "broil" and set an oven rack on the second-to-highest rung.

5. Lay shrimp on their sides on a baking sheet (if desired, line the baking sheet with foil or parchment paper). For even more spice, sprinkle over the optional chile.

6. Broil the shrimp 3 minutes per side. When turning, spoon over any leftover marinade from the bottom of the bowl.

7. Plate up the broiled shrimp and garnish with wedges of lemon or lime, plus a sprinkling of fresh coriander.

SEAFOOD

Fiery Garlic Shrimp

INGREDIENTS

2 ancho chiles, dried
1 chile de arbol, dried
$\frac{1}{2}$ cup tomato sauce
4 garlic cloves, peeled and crushed
$\frac{1}{4}$ cup chopped onion
1 lime, juiced
1 teaspoon white vinegar
2 tablespoons cooking oil
$\frac{1}{4}$ teaspoon salt (or more to taste)
25 large frozen shrimp, thawed, shelled and
  cleaned
1 green onion, chopped

YIELD: 2–3 SERVINGS

1. Cut the stems off of the dried chiles and slit
   them down the side. Shake them to remove
   the seeds.

2. Soak the chiles in hot water 30 minutes.
   Reserve $\frac{1}{2}$ cup soaking liquid.

3. In a blender, puree the chiles, tomato sauce,
   garlic, onion, lime juice, vinegar, oil, and salt
   into a sauce.

4. Place 5 shrimp on each skewer; baste with
   sauce. Grill over medium heat until done,
   about 4 minutes. Serve shrimp over a bed of

rice and top with a sprinkle of sliced green onion.

If you are using wooden skewers, soak them in warm water for 30 minutes to prevent them from scorching.

Garlic Shrimp and Fish Scampi

INGREDIENTS

1/4 cup unsalted butter
5 cloves garlic, minced
1 onion, minced
1/3 cup lemon juice
1 teaspoon grated lemon zest
1/8 teaspoon cayenne pepper
2 tablespoons dry white wine
1 teaspoon dried thyme leaves
4 (4-ounce) red snapper fillets
8 ounces medium raw shrimp, peeled
1 cup grape tomatoes
1/3 cup chopped parsley

YIELD: 4 SERVINGS

1. In large saucepan melt butter over medium-low heat. Add garlic and onion; cook and stir 6–8 minutes, until onion starts to brown.

2. Add lemon juice, zest, cayenne pepper, wine, and thyme; bring to a simmer. Simmer 2 minutes.

3. Add fillets; cook 2 minutes and turn. Add shrimp and grape tomatoes; cover and cook 3–5 minutes, shaking pan, until shrimp turn pink.

4. Uncover, stir gently, sprinkle with parsley, and serve immediately.

Quick Garlic Shrimp Stir-Fry

INGREDIENTS

1 tablespoon olive oil
3 cloves garlic, minced
$1/2$ pound jumbo shrimp, cleaned and deveined
Juice of $1/2$ lemon
Sea salt and freshly ground pepper, to taste
$1/2$ pound sugar snap peas, rinsed, ends chopped
  off
$1/4$ cup finely chopped fresh thyme
$1/3$ cup brown rice or rice noodles, cooked

YIELD: 2 SERVINGS

1. Heat oil in a wok or skillet over medium-high heat. Add garlic and sauté for a minute or less before adding shrimp. Be sure not to let garlic brown.

2. Pour in lemon juice and sprinkle in salt and pepper, stirring intermittently.

3. After 5-8 minutes, when the shrimp are starting to turn pink, toss in sugar snap peas and thyme.

4. Continue to stir for another 5-8 minutes for al dente peas, or longer if you prefer them softer. Serve over $1/3$ cup brown rice or rice noodles.

SEAFOOD

Grilled Shellfish with Garlic

INGREDIENTS

2 pounds mussels
2 pounds cherrystone clams
6 cups water
1/4 cup salt
1/4 cup butter
1/4 cup olive oil
1 onion, chopped
8 cloves garlic, minced
1 cup dry white wine
1/4 cup lemon juice
1/2 cup chopped cilantro

YIELD: 4 SERVINGS

1. Scrub mussels and clams; remove beards from mussels. Discard open shellfish. Soak in mixture of water and salt for 10 minutes.

2. Place roasting pan on grill over medium-high heat. Add butter and olive oil; heat for 2 minutes.

3. Add onion and garlic; cook and stir for 4-5 minutes. Add wine and lemon juice and bring to a simmer.

4. Add mussels and clams. Cover and grill for 8-12 minutes until shellfish open. Add to roasting pan and stir; garnish with cilantro and serve with dipping sauce.

Grilled Cheese and Herb Mussels with Garlic

INGREDIENTS

1/2 cup butter
7 cloves garlic, minced
1/4 cup lemon juice
1 cup grated Parmesan cheese
2 tablespoons chopped fresh thyme leaves
1/3 cup chopped flat-leaf parsley
4 pounds mussels

YIELD: 4 SERVINGS

1. In small saucepan, melt butter with garlic over low heat. Let simmer until garlic is fragrant, about 4 minutes.

2. Remove from heat and stir in lemon juice; set aside. Combine cheese, thyme, and parsley and place in several small bowls. Clean mussels and remove beards.

3. Arrange mussels directly on the grate over direct high heat, or place on a grill mat. Cover the grill and cook until the shells open, about 3–5 minutes.

4. Serve immediately with the butter sauce: Dip the mussels into sauce, then into the cheese herb mixture.

SEAFOOD

Cilantro-Garlic Steamed Clams

Cooking times will vary, depending on the size of the mollusks.

INGREDIENTS

2 dozen clams
4 tablespoons butter
6 cloves garlic, minced
1 teaspoon grated ginger root
1/2 cup minced cilantro
1 tablespoon dark sesame oil
1 tablespoon soy sauce
1/2 teaspoon rice wine vinegar
1/2 teaspoon lemon or lime zest
Salt and pepper to taste
1/2 cup rice wine
1/2 cup water or fish stock

YIELD: 4 SERVINGS

1. Carefully scrub clam shells to remove any dirt. Rinse with cold water.

2. In a saucepan combine butter, garlic, ginger, cilantro, sesame oil, soy sauce, vinegar, and zest. Season sauce with salt and pepper.

3. Heat sauce over medium-high heat, stirring often. Simmer 2 minutes, then remove from heat.

4. Place clams, hinge side down, in a steamer basket. Discard any open clams that don't close when tapped.

5. Pour wine and water or stock into a large saucepan that can accommodate the steamer basket.

6. Cover pot and place over high heat. Steam clams 6–8 minutes, or until clams open.

7. Remove clams to a serving bowl. Discard any that did not open.

8. Reduce steaming liquid by half; whisk into sauce. Serve clams with sauce.

Roasted Garlic Crab

INGREDIENTS

6 tablespoons (³/₄ stick) unsalted butter
6 tablespoons extra-virgin olive oil
2 tablespoons minced garlic
4 Dungeness crabs, about 1¼ pounds each (ask your supermarket or fish market to remove all the inedible parts)
Salt and freshly ground black pepper
3 tablespoons freshly squeezed lemon juice
¹/₃ cup finely chopped fresh Italian flat-leaf parsley

YIELD: 4 SERVINGS

1. Preheat the oven to 500°F.

2. Heat the butter, oil, and garlic in a very large ovenproof sauté pan over medium-high heat.

3. Rinse the crabs under cool running water. Add the crabs to the pan, season with salt and pepper to taste, and toss well. Transfer the pan to the oven; roast until the garlic turns light brown and the crab is heated through, about 12 minutes. Toss once halfway through.

4. Pour the crabs into a large warm serving bowl, add the lemon juice and parsley, and toss well.

> Garlic becomes sweet and tender when it's roasted because the compounds that make it taste so strong can no longer react after its cells have been heated. Garlic is very good for you. It contains high amounts of selenium, manganese, vitamin B6, and vitamin C. People who eat garlic every day may have a reduced risk of some diseases, including heart disease and stroke.

Garlic-Peppered Fish

INGREDIENTS

8 fish fillets, about 6 ounces each (rockfish, cod,
  halibut, or sea bass)
4 garlic cloves, peeled and minced
Juice from $\frac{1}{2}$ lemon
Salt and freshly ground pepper
$\frac{1}{2}$ cup (1 stick) butter, softened
3 tablespoons brandy
1 tablespoon green peppercorns, drained
$\frac{1}{4}$ cup olive oil
$\frac{1}{2}$ cup bread crumbs
Lemon slices, for garnish

YIELD: 8 SERVINGS

1. Sprinkle the fish with the garlic and lemon
   juice. Season with salt and pepper.

2. Preheat the oven to 400°F.

3. In a bowl, mix the butter with the brandy and
   peppercorns; season with salt and pepper.

4. Bake the fish on a preheated, oiled baking
   sheet for about 5 minutes.

5. Turn the fish over. Scatter bread crumbs
   and little dabs of flavored butter over each
   fillet. Bake the fish for another 6–8 minutes,
   or until cooked through. Garnish with lemon
   slices.

There are various tests to determine done-ness when you're cooking fish: If the fish is beginning to flake but not yet falling apart, it's ready. For boned fish, if you see the flesh separating from the bone, and the bone itself is no longer pink, it's done. If the flesh has turned from translucent to opaque (usually white), the fish is good to go.

Baby Artichokes with Aioli

INGREDIENTS

12 baby artichokes
1 tablespoon plus 1 cup olive oil, divided
1 tablespoon Italian seasoning
Salt
$1/2$ teaspoon freshly ground black pepper
6 garlic cloves
2 large egg yolks
1 lemon, juiced
1 teaspoon Dijon mustard
1 tablespoon balsamic vinegar
White pepper
Parmesan, shredded

YIELD: 4 SERVINGS

1. Pull off the tough outer leaves of the artichokes. Trim the stems, keeping them as long as possible. Cut off the prickly leaf tips with kitchen scissors and slice the artichokes in half with a large knife.

2. Cover the artichokes with water in a large pot with 1 tablespoon olive oil, the Italian seasoning, 1 teaspoon salt, and the black pepper. Steam until tender, about 25 minutes.

3. Puree the garlic cloves in a food processor or blender.

4. In a small bowl, whisk the egg yolks until smooth. Add the yolks, lemon juice, mustard, vinegar, and salt and white pepper (to taste) to the pureed garlic.

5. While the processor is running, add 1 cup olive oil in a slow, steady stream. Blend until thick and shiny. The aioli can be refrigerated for up to 4 hours.

6. Using tongs, remove the artichokes from the water. Place on a lightly oiled baking sheet. Drizzle with the aioli, sprinkle with the Parmesan, and place under broiler for 5 minutes.

Eggplant with Garlic Sauce

INGREDIENTS

4 small Asian eggplants
Vegetable oil for frying
3 tablespoons soy sauce
3 tablespoons rice wine vinegar
3 tablespoons sugar
1 tablespoon rice wine
1 green onion, minced
1 tablespoon minced ginger root
6 cloves garlic, minced
1 tablespoon minced fermented black beans
1 teaspoon hot chile paste
1 tablespoon dark sesame oil
1 tablespoon cornstarch dissolved in 2
   tablespoons cold water

YIELD: 4 SERVINGS

1. Trim top and bottom tips from eggplants;
   discard. Cut eggplants into 1½-inch pieces.

2. Pour oil in wok to a depth of 2 inches;
   heat until hot. Fry eggplant. Drain all but 2
   tablespoons oil.

3. In a bowl, whisk together soy sauce, vinegar,
   sugar, and wine.

4. Stir-fry green onion, ginger, garlic, black beans, chile paste, and sesame oil over high heat 20 seconds. Add eggplant and sauce to wok. Stir-fry 30 seconds. Add dissolved cornstarch to wok and cook until sauce is thick. Serve.

Mexican Garlic Rice

INGREDIENTS

3 garlic cloves, finely chopped
1/4 medium onion
2 tablespoons cooking oil
1 1/2 cups rice
2 1/2 cups chicken broth
1 cup tomato sauce
4 heaping tablespoons finely chopped parsley
  (optional)

YIELD: 4–6 SERVINGS

1. Sauté the garlic and onion in the oil over medium heat 2–3 minutes, until onions are softened.

2. Add rice and stir about 5 minutes, until rice becomes a golden brown color.

3. Carefully add broth and tomato sauce; stir and bring to a boil. Once mixture starts to boil, turn heat to low and cover; simmer 20 minutes.

4. Fluff the rice with a fork and fold in the parsley. Serve immediately.

Scalloped Potatoes with Garlic

INGREDIENTS

¹/₄ cup unsalted butter
1 onion, chopped
5 cloves garlic, minced
¹/₄ cup flour
¹/₂ teaspoon dry mustard
¹/₈ teaspoon salt

¼ teaspoon pepper
1 tablespoon fresh oregano
2 cups 1 percent milk
1 cup light cream
⅓ cup sour cream
6 russet potatoes, peeled and sliced ⅛-inch
thick

YIELD: 6-8 SERVINGS

1. In saucepan, melt butter over medium heat. Add onion and garlic; cook and stir 7 minutes.

2. Add flour, mustard, salt, and pepper; cook and stir 5 minutes. Add oregano, milk, and cream; bring to a simmer.

3. Simmer sauce until thickened, stirring constantly. Add sour cream.

4. Layer ⅓ potatoes in greased 2-quart baking dish; top with ⅓ sauce; repeat layers. Bake at 325°F 60-70 minutes until potatoes are tender.

If you're feeding a crowd, make two or three pans of this recipe. Store them well covered in the refrigerator up to 8 hours. Then bake as directed, adding 15-20 minutes to the baking time.

Garlicky Hasselback Potatoes

INGREDIENTS

6 russet potatoes
8 cups water
2 cups ice
6 cloves garlic, minced
1/4 cup unsalted butter
2 tablespoons lemon juice
1 teaspoon dried Italian seasoning
1/4 teaspoon pepper
3 tablespoons grated Parmesan cheese
1 cup panko bread crumbs

YIELD: 6 SERVINGS

1. Peel potatoes, placing in a mixture of water and ice cubes as you work.

2. Cook garlic in butter 4–5 minutes over low heat. Remove from heat.

3. Place potatoes in large spoon. Make crosswise slices across the potato, 1/8-inch apart and not all the way through.

4. Place potatoes in pan. Mix garlic butter, juice, seasoning, and pepper; drizzle on potatoes. Bake at 400°F 40 minutes. Mix cheese and bread crumbs; sprinkle on potatoes. Bake 25–35 minutes until golden.

Garlic and Edamame Risotto

INGREDIENTS

5 cups vegetable broth
1 cup water
2 tablespoons olive oil
1 onion, finely chopped
3 cloves garlic, minced
1½ cups Arborio rice
½ cup dry white wine
3 cups frozen edamame, thawed

¼ cup butter
½ cup grated Parmesan cheese

YIELD: 4 SERVINGS

1. In medium saucepan, combine vegetable broth and water; heat over low heat.

2. In large saucepan, heat oil over medium heat. Add onion and garlic; cook and stir for 6 minutes.

3. Add rice; cook and stir for 3–4 minutes. Add wine; cook and stir until absorbed. Gradually add the hot broth mixture, ½ cup at a time, stirring constantly.

4. After 20 minutes, the rice should be al dente and the sauce creamy. Stir in edamame, butter, and cheese; cover; cook 3–4 minutes, then stir and serve.

> If there's one secret to risotto, it's to stir the rice almost constantly with a metal spoon.
>
> The physical manipulation of the rice helps break down its cells, which lets the starch release into the cooking liquid.

Garlicky Red Beans and Rice

INGREDIENTS

2 tablespoons olive oil
1 onion, chopped
4 cloves garlic, minced
3 cups vegetable broth
$\frac{1}{2}$ cup water
$1\frac{1}{2}$ cups medium-grain rice
2 (15-ounce) cans kidney beans
1 cup chopped celery
1 red bell pepper, chopped
$\frac{1}{2}$ teaspoon dried oregano leaves
$\frac{1}{3}$ cup chopped fresh cilantro
$\frac{1}{4}$ teaspoon Tabasco sauce
Salt and pepper to taste

YIELD: 6 SERVINGS

1. In microwave-safe casserole, combine olive oil, onion, and garlic. Microwave on high for 3–4 minutes until tender.

2. Stir in vegetable broth and water along with rice. Cover and microwave on high for 14–18 minutes until rice is almost tender.

3. Drain beans and rinse; drain again. Stir into rice mixture along with remaining ingredients.

4. Microwave, uncovered, on high for 2–3 minutes, stirring once, until rice is tender and mixture is hot. Let stand for 5 minutes, then serve.

BOOKS

Gilroy Garlic Festival Staff. *The Garlic Lovers'
Cookbook, Vol. II,* Celestial Arts, 2005.
For more garlic recipes check out this tome by the
people behind the Garlic Capital of the World.

Lau, Benjamin. *Garlic and You: The Modern Medicine,* Apple Publishing Company, 1999. Learn how garlic can help reduce stress, slow the aging process, and protect against allergies.

Meredith, Ted Jordan. *The Complete Book of Garlic,* Timber Press, 2008. Explores the health benefits, culinary uses, and profiles of garlic along with instructions for growing your own.

WEB SITES

AllRecipes.com
http://allrecipes.com
This site features reader-submitted recipes that are rated by members. Recipes can be filtered by ingredient using the search feature.

Bon Appétit
www.bonappetit.com
Always features a variety of dishes with a unique spin on everyday ingredients like garlic.

Ciao Italia

www.ciaoitalia.com

A focus on all things Italian.

Cooks.com

www.cooks.com

Any and all recipes, vegetable and otherwise, along with many tips, nutrition facts, and forums.

Epicurious

www.epicurious.com

Find virtually any garlic recipe here, with helpful slideshows and commentary.

Food Network

www.foodnetwork.com

Like the TV shows, the Web site for the food network is packed with information, from recipes to techniques.

The Garlic Store

www.thegarlicstore.com

For all of your garlic needs, from fresh garlic and garlic presses to garlic sauces and spices.

Whole Foods Market
www.wholefoodsmarket.com/recipes
Search for delicious garlic recipes and new
inspirations for using your favorite ingredient

Aioli: A garlic mayonnaise made in France's Provence region, used as a condiment or sauce.

Baste: To brush cooking food with a liquid to keep it moist as it roasts or bakes.

Broil: To cook food close to the heat source, quickly.

Chop: To cut food into small pieces, using a chef's knife or a food processor.

Cornish hen: A very young chicken, sold whole. Usually stuffed or roasted.

Direct grilling: To cook food directly over a heat source, whether a burner, coals, or burning wood.

Dredge: To evenly coat poultry or meat with flour.

Drip pan: A pan used in grilling, usually made of aluminum, placed in the coal bed under the food to catch drips as the food cooks over indirect heat.

Drippings: Brown bits made of meat, skin, and fat left in the pan after meat is browned.

Grill: To cook over coals or charcoal, or over high heat.

Indirect grilling: To cook food over an area on the grill where there are no coals, usually over a drip pan.

Julienne: To cut food into thin strips, also called matchsticks.

Marinate: To allow meats or vegetables to stand in a mixture of an acid and oil, to add flavor and tenderize.

Sauté: To cook food briefly in oil over medium-high heat, while stirring it so it cooks evenly.

Seasoning: To add herbs, spices, citrus juices and zest, and peppers to food to increase flavor.

Slow cooker: An appliance that cooks food by surrounding it with low, steady heat.

Spatchcocked: A technique that removes the backbone and flattens chicken so it is easily grilled.

Steam: To cook food by immersing it in steam. Food is set over boiling liquid.

Stir-fry: To quickly cook food by manipulating it with a spoon or spatula, in a wok or pan, over high heat.

Toss: To combine food using two spoons or a spoon and a fork until mixed well.

Truss: To tie meat or poultry with string to maintain its shape during the cooking process.

Wood chips: Chips of real wood, sometimes flavored, soaked and added to the fire to add flavor to grilled food ●

APPROXIMATE U.S.–METRIC EQUIVALENTS

LIQUID INGREDIENTS

U.S. Measures	Metric	U.S. Measures	Metric
1/4 tsp.	1.23 ml	2 Tbsp.	29.57 ml
1/2 tsp.	2.36 ml	3 Tbsp.	44.36 ml
3/4 tsp.	3.70 ml	1/4 cup	59.15 ml
1 tsp.	4.93 ml	1/2 cup	118.30 ml
1 1/4 tsp.	6.16 ml	1 cup	236.59 ml
1 1/2 tsp.	7.39 ml	2 cups or 1 pt.	473.18 ml
1 3/4 tsp.	8.63 ml	3 cups	709.77 ml
2 tsp.	9.86 ml	4 cups or 1 qt.	946.36 ml
1 Tbsp.	14.79 ml	4 qts. or 1 gal.	3.79 l

DRY INGREDIENTS

U.S. Measures	Metric	U.S. Measures		Metric
1/16 oz.	2 (1.8) g	2 4/5 oz.		80 g
1/8 oz.	3 1/2 (3.5) g	3 oz.		85 (84.9) g
1/4 oz.	7 (7.1) g	3 1/2 oz.		100 g
1/2 oz.	15 (14.2) g	4 oz.		115 (113.2) g
3/4 oz.	21 (21.3) g	4 1/2 oz.		125 g
7/8 oz.	25 g	5 1/4 oz.		150 g
1 oz.	30 (28.3) g	8 7/8 oz.		250 g
1 3/4 oz.	50 g	16 oz.	1 Lb.	454 g
2 oz.	60 (56.6) g	17 3/5 oz.	1 Livre	500 g

adobo sauce, 58
Alfredo sauce, 14
almonds, 40
Anaheim chiles, 18, 20
ancho chiles, 72
appetizers, 8–31
apple cider vinegar, 58, 68
Arborio rice, 104
artichoke, 14, 90
Asian eggplant, 92

Baby Artichokes with Aioli,
    90–91
bacon, 30
balsamic vinegar, 9, 90
bamboo shoots, 60
barbecue sauce, 58
basil, 44
bay leaves, 26, 43
beef, 52–59
bell pepper, 18, 30, 40, 63, 106
black beans, 10, 56, 92
black olives, 40
blue cheese, 52
bok choy, 62
brandy, 86
bread crumbs, 86, 102
bread, Italian, 24
Brie cheese, 13
broccoli, 89
Broccoli with Garlic Sauce, 89
brown rice, 77
brown sugar, 42, 70
Bruschetta, 24
brussel sprouts, 94, 95
Brussel Sprouts with Garlic,
    94–95

carrots, 26, 27, 48, 67
casserole, 40–41
cayenne pepper, 38, 43,
    70, 74
celery, 106
celery leaves, 32
charcoal, 49
cherrystone clams, 78
chicken, 10, 28, 30, 32–33, 34,
    36, 38–39, 40–41, 42–43
Chicken Adobo with Garlic,
    42–43
chicken broth, 30, 32, 39, 42,
    51, 97, 98
chicken stock, 8, 10, 40, 48
chicken thighs, 40
chicken wings, 28, 29, 30
Chicken with 40 Cloves of
    Garlic, 32–33
chile de arbol, 72
chile flakes, 70
chile paste, 56, 60, 92
chile, red, 70
chiles, 18, 19, 20, 70, 72
chiles, ancho, 72
chili powder, 58, 97
chopping garlic, 1–2
cider vinegar, 58, 68
cilantro, 10, 18, 20, 22, 78,
    82, 106
Cilantro-Garlic Steamed
    Clams, 82–83
cinnamon, 40
clams, 78, 82
coconut milk, 42, 70
cod, 86
compound butter, 53

corn, 10, 63
Cornish game hens, 44, 46–47
cornstarch, 56, 60, 62, 92
crabs, 84
cream, light, 101
cumin, 10, 97
curry powder, 28

Dijon mustard, 64, 68, 90
dips, 14, 16
dry mustard, 34, 66, 100
Dungeness crab, 84

Easy Chili-Garlic Shrimp, 70–71
edamame, 104
Eggplant with Garlic Sauce, 92–93
eggplant, 92

Fiery Garlic Shrimp, 72–73
fish, cooking, 87
fish fillet, 86
fish sauce, 70
fish stock, 82
flank steak, 56

Garlic and Edamame Risotto, 104–5
Garlic Chicken Casserole, 40–41
Garlic Chicken Paprikash, 38–39
Garlic Curried Wings, 28–29
Garlic Sage Turkey, 50–51

Garlic Shrimp and Fish Scampi, 74–75
Garlic Wings Casino, 30–31
Garlic-Lemon Marinated Grilled Chops, 64
Garlic-Peppered Fish, 86–87
Garlicky Hasselback Potatoes, 102
Garlicky Pinto Beans, 97
Garlicky Red Beans and Rice, 106–7
Garlicky Salsa Verde, 20–21
ginger root, 82, 92
grill seasoning, 53
Grilled Cheese and Herb Mussels with Garlic, 81
Grilled Shellfish with Garlic, 78
Grilled Steak with Garlic-Lemon Paste, 55
grilling, 36, 44, 45, 48–49, 52–53, 55, 58–59, 64, 68–69, 72–73, 78, 81

halibut, 86
Havarti cheese, 14
Herbed Pork Roast with Garlic, 66–67
honey, 28, 44, 68
Hot and Spicy Short Ribs, 58–59

Italian bread, 24
Italian dressing, 90
Italian seasoning, 102

jalapeño, 22, 26, 97

kaffir lime leaves, 70
kidney beans, 106

leek, 8, 14, 56
lemon zest, 44, 48, 64, 74, 82
Lemon-Garlic Grilled Hens, 44, 45
Lemon-Garlic Roasted Turkey, 48–49
lime, 70, 72
lime juice, 20, 22
lime leaves, 70
lime zest, 82

Manchego cheese, 40
marjoram, 55
Mexican Garlic Rice, 98
mincing garlic, 3
mushroom, wood ear, 60
mushrooms, 60, 62
mussels, 78, 81

olives, 40
onion powder, 97
oregano, 32, 44, 52, 64, 101, 106

pancetta, 8
panko bread crumbs, 102
paprika, 32, 34, 36, 38, 40, 46, 55, 66
Parmesan cheese, 9, 14, 30, 81, 90, 94, 102, 105
parsley, 32, 74, 81, 84, 98
peeling garlic, 1, 17
peppercorn, 26, 56, 86

Pickled Carrots with Garlic, 26, 27
Pico de Gallo, 22–23
pimento, 40
pinto beans, 97
pork, 60–69
pork butt, 60
pork chops, 64, 65
pork loin, 60
pork loin roast, 66, 68
Pork Roast with Garlic and Rosemary, 68–69
pork tenderloin, 62
potatoes, 67, 101, 102
poultry, 32–51
poultry seasoning, 50

Quick Garlic Shrimp Stir-Fry, 77

red bell pepper, 18, 40, 106
red chile, 70
red snapper, 74
red wine, 8
red wine vinegar, 9
rib eye steak, 52, 55
Rib Eye with Roasted Garlic Butter, 52–53
rice, 40, 43, 77, 98, 104, 106
rice, brown, 77
rice, long-grain, 40, 43
rice, medium-grain, 106
rice noodles, 77
rice wine, 56, 60, 62, 82, 92
rice wine vinegar, 60, 82, 92
Rich Artichoke Garlic Dip, 14

risotto, 104–5
Roast Lemon-Garlic
    Chicken, 34
Roasted Chile Salsa with
    Garlic, 18–19
Roasted Garlic Cornish
    Hens, 46–47
Roasted Garlic Crab, 84–85
Roasted Garlic Dip, 16
Roasted Garlic Herb
    Spread, 13
Roasted Garlic Tortilla
    Soup, 10–11
roasting garlic, 4, 6
rockfish, 86
rosemary, 16, 66, 68
russet potatoes, 101, 102

sage, 50
salsa, 18–19, 20–21
sauce: adobo, 58; Alfredo,
    14; barbecue sauce, 58;
    Broccoli with Garlic, 89;
    Eggplant with Garlic,
    92–93; fish, 70; Shredded
    Pork in Garlic, 60–61
sautéing garlic, 4
Scalloped Potatoes with
    Garlic, 100–101
seafood, 70–87
sea bass, 86
sesame oil, 56, 60, 82, 92
shallot, 28, 94
shiitake mushrooms, 62
short ribs, 58
Shredded Pork in Garlic
    Sauce, 60–61

shrimp, 70, 72, 74, 77
shrimp paste, 70
side dishes, 89–107
sirloin steak, 56
Sliced Beef with Garlic and
    Leeks, 56–57
soup, 8, 10
sour cream, 10, 13, 16,
    39, 101
soy sauce, 42, 56, 58, 60, 62,
    82, 90
spatchcock, 37
Spatchcocked Grilled Chicken
    with Garlic Marinade, 36
spinach, 14
spreads, 13
steak, 52–53, 55, 56
Stir-Fried Garlic Pork
    Tenderloin, 62–63
storing garlic, 6
sugar snap peas, 77
Szechwan peppercorn, 56

Tabasco sauce, 106
Three-Onion Soup with
    Garlic, 8–9
thyme, 32, 40, 46, 47, 48, 66,
    74, 77, 81
tomatillos, 20
tomato sauce, 72, 98
tomatoes, 10, 18, 22, 39,
    40, 74
tortilla chips, 10
turkey, 48, 50, 51

vegetable broth, 104, 106
vinegar, balsamic, 9, 90

vinegar, red wine, 9
vinegar, rice wine, 60, 82, 92

water chestnut, 60, 63
white sauce, 14
white wine, 30, 32, 42, 47, 74,
    78, 104

wine vinegar, 42
wok, cooking, 56–57, 60–61,
    62–63, 77, 92–93
wood chips, 58, 68
wood ear mushroom, 60